99 WAYS TO OPEN A BEER BOTTLE
WITHOUT A BOTTLE OPENER

Brett Stern

CHRONICLE BOOKS

SAN FRANCISCO

Copyright © 2014 by Brett Stern.

Library of Congress Cataloging-in-Publication Data:

Stern, Brett.
  99 ways to open a beer bottle without a bottle opener / Brett Stern.
     pages cm
  ISBN 978-1-4521-3259-4
  1. American wit and humor. I. Title. II. Title: Ninety-nine ways to open a beer bottle without a bottle opener.

  PN6162.S825 2014
  818'.5402—dc23

                                    2013038356

Manufactured in China

Designed by Liam Flanagan

10 9 8 7 6 5 4 3 2

Chronicle Books LLC
680 Second Street
San Francisco, California 94107
www.chroniclebooks.com

"I don't think there is any other quality so essential to success of any kind as the quality of perseverance. It overcomes everything, even nature."

—JOHN D. ROCKEFELLER

INTRODUCTION

Right about now, an icy cold bottle of beer sounds awesome. But an icy cold bottle of beer in hand that's not a twist off—with no bottle opener in sight—sounds like a disaster.

Worry not, fellow beer drinkers: life's too short to let such trivial things keep you from your brew. After years of trial and error and enough beer drinking, I've put together this handy how-to reference guide to solve all of your problems, or rather that most crucial problem of getting your beer open without an opener, no matter where you are or what you might have at hand.

In life, sometimes you don't have the correct tool to complete a task. But with the easy-to-follow photographs and instructions in this book, you'll be quenching your thirst in no time. As you use and apply these methods, you will soon recognize the possible variations, adapt them to come up with your own solutions, and attain the rank of Professional Beer Bottle Opener. Let's face it, all you're doing is prying a round piece of metal off a round piece of glass. Cheers!

Why is my beer capped like this in the first place?

In 1892, William Painter, a mechanical engineer and foreman in a machine shop, was hired by a bottle manufacturer to develop a universal neck size and shape for glass bottles. These bottles were to be used for carbonated beverages and beer to standardize production and quality control. Having accomplished this, he then recognized the need for a uniform cap for the bottles, and patented the "crown cork cap" as a sealing method. These innovations allowed for the invention of a machine to fill the bottles with liquid and carbonation, a machine for securing or "crowning" the caps on the bottles, and of course the bottle cap opener. A prolific inventor with eighty-five patents, Painter was inducted into the Inventors Hall of Fame in 2006.

To accompany each method, I have instituted a skill-rating system indicating the degree of difficulty.

I wish you luck and happy beer drinking!

ALWAYS REMEMBER: *Never drink from a bottle if you break the glass.*

Do you have your own unique method?
Email me a photo at open@99openbeers.com.

EDGE OF TABLE

1 Place cap on edge of table

2 Just punch the sh*t out of it

3 Drink the rewards

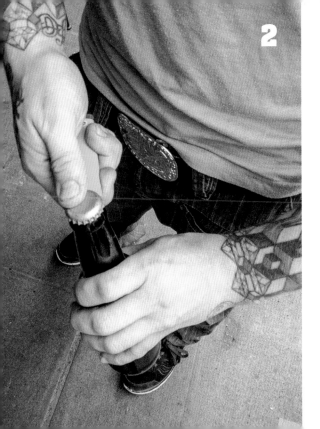

DISPOSABLE LIGHTER

1. Hold bottle securely
2. Place bottom of lighter under cap
3. Place thumb on top of cap
4. Pry off cap
5. Drink
6. You are a professional

BOTTLE TO BOTTLE

1. Hold cap to cap
2. Pull apart, trying to get the bottom bottle to open first
3. Drink

Beware: Due to Murphy's Law, the top bottle usually opens first. If the beer gods are smiling on you, both beers will open without spilling a drop.

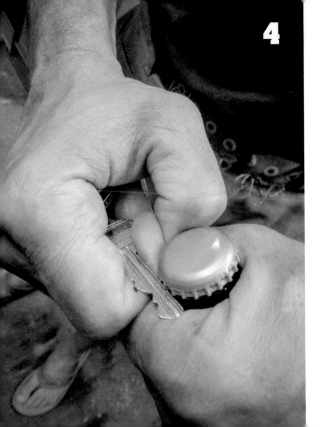

KEY

1 Place end of key under cap

2 Pry off cap

3 Drink

4 Don't lose your keys

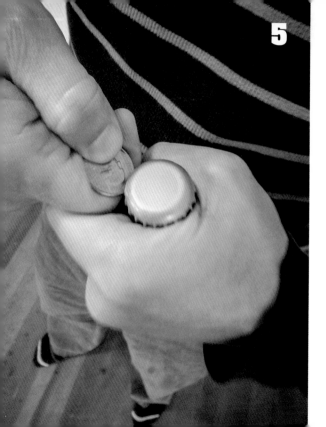

POCKET CHANGE

1. Spend the last of your cash on cheap beer

2. Reach into your pockets and realize you have spare change

3. While holding bottle securely, place lucky coin under cap

4. Pop off cap

5. Drink

CORKSCREW

1. First of all, why do you have a corkscrew and not a bottle opener?
2. Place tip of corkscrew under cap rim
3. Pry off cap
4. Drink beer not wine

PROPANE TANK

1. Go to store to refill grill's propane tank

2. Pick up another six-pack of beer

3. Carry tank home and notice the metal frame of the hand support is a perfect bottle opener

4. Pry off cap

5. Drink

6. Enjoy the BBQ

BBQ GRILL

1 Stick cap in grill

2 Press down

3 Pour some beer on steaks

4 Drink

5 Don't forget to flip the meat

PACKAGED ICE COOLER

1 Case of beer: check

2 Bag of chips: check

3 Bag of ice: check

4 Wedge cap under door

5 Pry off cap

6 Drink

BEER KEG TAP

Eventually the keg will be empty.

1 Collect some coin and do a quick beer run

2 Place cap in tap/keg connector

3 Pry off cap

4 Drink

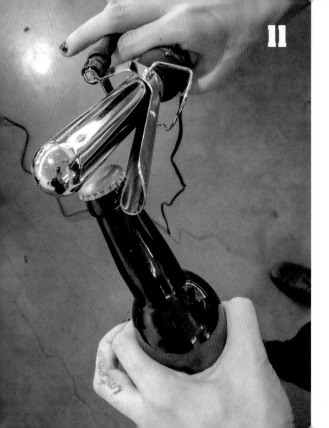

CURLING IRON

1 Before turning iron on, place cap between iron and curling bar

2 Pry off cap

3 Drink

4 Turn iron on

5 Drink

6 Curl hair

7 Drink

EYELASH CURLER

1. Get ready for a fun night out
2. Place metal lip under cap
3. Gently lift up
4. Drink
5. Redo your lipstick

DOOR KNOCKER

1 Bring a six-pack to friend's house to watch the game

2 Knock on front door with knocker

3 Realize six-pack is getting heavy

4 Remove one bottle and place cap under knocker

5 Press down to open

6 Drink

7 Decide to try doorbell

DOOR STRIKE PLATE

1 Place cap in lock opening

2 Pry off cap

3 Drink

DRUMS

1. Play a five minute solo
2. Place cap in between drum and metal lug
3. Pry off cap
4. Drink

DRUMSTICK

1. Practice, practice, practice
2. Take a break
3. Grab a cold beer
4. Place drumstick tip under cap and pop off
5. Drink
6. More cowbell

UPS TRUCK

1. There's always a UPS truck somewhere on the street

2. Place cap between back bumper supports

3. Pry off cap

4. Drink

FEDEX BOX

1. Quick, finish contract
2. Rush down to corner drop box just before pickup time
3. Drop envelope in box
4. Place cap between door and frame
5. Pry off cap
6. Celebrate
7. Drink

STAPLE REMOVER

1. Make fifty copies of your business plan and staple
2. Discover you left out a page
3. Find staple remover
4. Find beer
5. Place teeth over cap crown
6. Pry off cap
7. Drink
8. Insert missing page and restaple

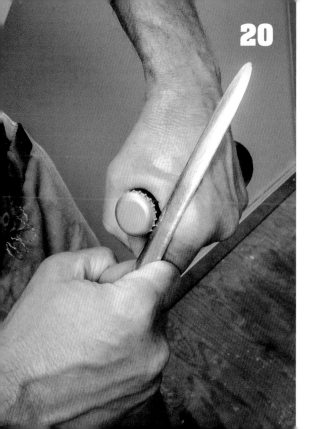

LETTER OPENER

1. Place blade of opener under cap
2. Try not to stab yourself
3. Pry off cap
4. Drink

FILE CABINET

1. Close office door
2. Place cap in draw pull
3. Press down
4. Hide from boss
5. Drink

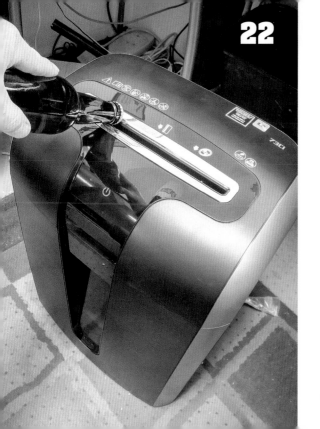

PAPER SHREDDER

1. Quick—shred the evidence
2. Place cap in shredding slot
3. Pry off cap
4. Drink and celebrate your continued freedom

MOVIE KIOSK (DATE NIGHT)

1. Go to supermarket to get a movie and beer
2. Decide between an action adventure or romantic comedy
3. Place beer in movie pickup slot
4. Press down
5. Drink
6. Go home and enjoy the movie

VENDING MACHINE

1 Place cap in coin slot

2 Press down

3 Drink

MACBOOK CHARGER

1. Remove outlet plug adapter from charger*

2. Place connector pin under cap

3. Gently pry up

4. Drink

5. Steve Jobs really was a genius

* Will also work with iPad charger.

CAMERA

1. Buy an expensive camera
2. Place cap in flash hot shoe
3. Gently pry cap off metal frame
4. Drink
5. Turn on auto focus and shoot some pictures

POOL BRIDGE

1 Bet double or nothing you can open beer using something on pool table

2 Get pool bridge kept on side of pool table

3 Place cap in bridge opening

4 Press down

5 Don't spill any beer on the felt

6 Win the bet

7 Drink

PING-PONG PADDLE

1 Hit final kill shot to win match

2 Grab a beer and place paddle handle under cap

3 Pop cap off

4 Be a good sport and open another for your opponent

5 Drink

TV REMOTE CONTROL

1 Lie on couch watching the game

2 Get up during commercial for another beer

3 Lie back down, realize you didn't open beer

4 Find TV remote on coffee table

5 Place remote under cap and pop off*

6 Drink

* If you can do this while still lying on couch and not spilling on yourself, you are a pro.

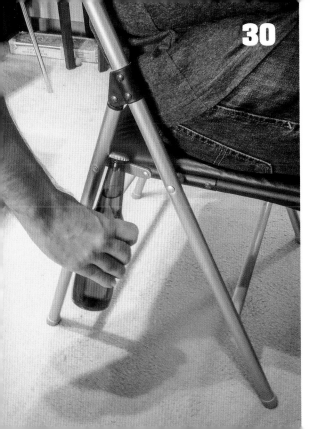

FOLDING CHAIR

You need to be sitting down for this method.

1 Place cap in chair hinge

2 Pry up

3 Drink

Hopefully the rest of the beer is on the table so you won't have to get up.

BABY CARRIAGE

1. Take baby out for a stroll
2. Give baby his bottle
3. Pull out your own bottle
4. Open off carriage frame
5. Drink
6. Finish your walk

WHEELCHAIR

1. Hold beer securely
2. Pry off metal frame
3. Drink

SECURITY GATE

1. Find metal security gate with openings in design
2. Find a place to wedge cap
3. Press down
4. Drink

BRICK WALL

1. Find wall to lean against
2. Place cap in between two bricks
3. Gently pry up
4. Drink
5. Just hang out for a while

CHAIN-LINK FENCE

1 Place cap between fence and metal pole

2 Press down

3 Drink

SURVEILLANCE SIGN

1 Wedge cap between chain-link fence and metal sign

2 Press down

3 Something tells me you are being watched, so don't drink here

BICYCLE GEAR

1. Finish twenty-five mile bike ride
2. Wedge cap in gear
3. Press down
4. Drink
5. Tell everyone you rode fifty miles

BICYCLE U-LOCK

1. Get off bike
2. Open U-lock and place cap in notch of U-bar
3. Pry up
4. Drink
5. Don't forget to lock up your bike

LOCK SHACKLE

1 Unlock door

2 Place cap in latch opening

3 Pry off cap

4 Drink

5 Don't forget to re-lock door

ROLLERBLADE

1. Place cap in between shoe and blade
2. Pry off cap
3. Drink
4. Try to keep your balance

SKATEBOARD

1. Place cap between truck and kingpin
2. Pry off cap
3. Drink
4. Attempt a 720-degree Gazelle Flip

SKI BINDING

1. Ski all day
2. Go to lodge
3. Lean ski against wall
4. Place cap in binding
5. Press down
6. Drink
7. Try not to break your leg when you go back out

TAPE DISPENSER

1. Finish packing boxes for end of day pickup
2. Grab a beer and trusty tape dispenser
3. Pop off cap
4. Drink

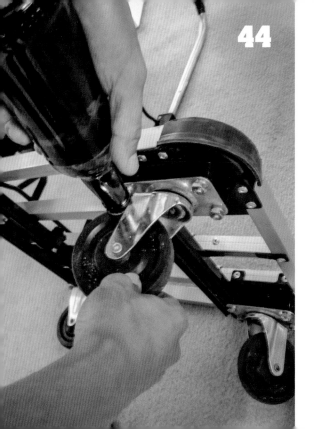

MOVING DOLLY

1. Beg your friends to help you move
2. Buy a case of beer
3. Move all your stuff
4. Place moving dolly on its side
5. Insert cap in wheel support
6. Press down
7. Drinks all around

TROPHY

1 Place cap in between legs of metal trophy you won

2 Pry off cap

3 Drink

4 Recount story about your big win

CHEWBACCA

1. Appreciate that your loyal first mate is always by your side, to protect and help you in any situation

2. Place Chewie's head under bottle cap

3. Pry off cap

4. Drink

5. Share with your best friend

GARAGE DOOR

1. Open garage door
2. Place cap in slot of door rail
3. Pry off cap
4. Drink
5. Don't forget to close the garage door

TOOL CHEST

1. Go to shop to work and get a beer

2. Remember you need special tool to open your beer

3. Something in your tool chest has to work

4. Try placing cap under drawer pull

5. Press down

6. Drink

CHANNELLOCK PLIERS

1 Try to fix the clogged drain

2 Decide to take a break and get an icy cold beer from fridge

3 Grip cap with pliers and pry off

4 Try again to fix the clogged drain

5 Decide again to take a break and get an icy cold beer from fridge

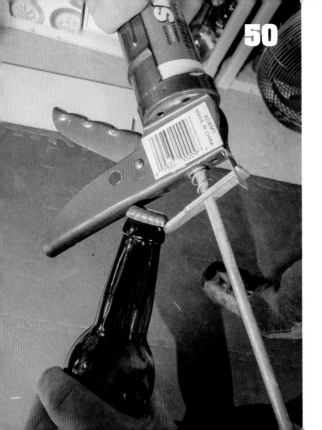

CAULKING GUN

1. Start "honey do" list
2. Try to remember where you left the caulking gun
3. Find the caulking gun
4. Realize the game will start in five minutes
5. Get beer
6. Open beer
7. Drink
8. Watch game and vow to finish list next weekend

SQUARE LAYOUT TOOL

1 Wedge cap in metal slot

2 Pry off cap

3 Drink

4 Use square to make sure everything is square

VICE

1 Open vice about ½ inch

2 Wedge cap in opening

3 Pry off cap

4 Drink

HAMMER

1. Place claw under cap lip
2. Pry off cap
3. Drink
4. Do not try hammering anything right now

NAIL

1. Tap nail with bottle bottom to bend it toward wall

2. Stick cap under nail

3. Press down

4. Drink

BELT BUCKLE

1 Undo buckle (don't let your pants fall down)

2 Place cap in buckle

3 Pry off cap

4 Drink

5 Don't forget to buckle up

WATCH

1. Check watch to make sure it's past noon somewhere on the planet
2. Remove watch
3. Grab beer securely
4. Place metal bezel under cap and above knuckle
5. Pop off cap
6. Drink

HAND GRENADE

1. Hold grenade securely
2. Place cap in grenade handle
3. Pry off cap
4. DO NOT PULL PIN!!!!
5. Drink

BRASS KNUCKLES

1. Two best friends
2. One bottle of beer
3. One set of brass knuckles
4. Decide between your-selves who gets the beer
5. Pry off cap
6. Drink

WATER TOWER

1. Find a six-story water tower

2. Somewhere on this large metal object there has to be a place to open your beer

3. Wedge cap into frame

4. Press down

5. Drink

RAILROAD ANCHOR PIN

1. Find yourself on the wrong side of the tracks with a beer

2. Place cap under metal pin

3. Pry off cap

4. Drink

5. Watch for trains

6. Keep on walking down the line

CANDELABRA

1. Get out into wilderness for some backcountry camping

2. Don't forget to bring your candelabra

3. Pry off metal frame

4. Drink

5. Put another log on the fire

FLASK

1. Always carry a full flask with you
2. Find an icy cold beer
3. Pry bottle cap off flask cap hinge
4. Drink
5. You now have a party in both hands!

BOAT ANCHOR

1. Get invited to sail on a friend's boat
2. Bring a cooler full of beer
3. Open beer off anchor
4. Get ready to cast off
5. Don't forget to untie boat from dock
6. Drink
7. Don't pilot boat

FAN

1 Find a cool place to hang out

2 Find a cold beer to enjoy

3 Pry cap off metal wire frame

4 Drink

5 Don't move from that spot

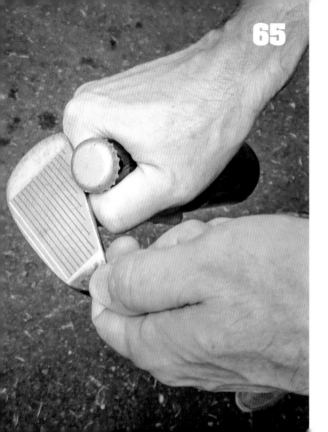

GOLF CLUB

1. Select iron of your choice
2. Place thumb under cap for leverage
3. Place club on top of thumb and under cap
4. Press up with club to remove cap
5. Drink
6. Try really hard to get the ball in the hole

66

CAR DOOR LATCH

1. Open door
2. Place cap in latch opening
3. Press down
4. Drink
5. Don't drive

HOOD ORNAMENT

1. Find an old pickup truck with any ornament bolted to its hood
2. Place cap in ornament's mouth
3. Pry off cap
4. Drink

LAWN LION

1. Quietly approach lion
2. Place cap in lion's mouth
3. Pull up to remove cap
4. Drink
5. Pet lion

LAWN MOWER

1. Place cap between frame and support
2. Press down
3. Drink
4. Now get back to work—that lawn is not going to mow itself

RAKE

1. Notice leaves have fallen in the backyard
2. Grab beer from fridge
3. Get rake from garage
4. Use giant bottle opener to pry off cap
5. Take a sip
6. Start raking the leaves
7. Take a sip
8. Keep raking the leaves

HOSE SPRAY NOZZLE

1. Water lawn
2. Realize you have a free hand
3. Grab a beer and place cap between spray handle and metal body
4. Pry off cap
5. Drink
6. Continue watering lawn

MANURE SHOVEL

1. Take a break from shoveling that pile of sh*t

2. Wash hands

3. Grab a cold beer

4. Place cap under metal lip of shovel

5. Drink

6. Now get back to shoveling sh*t

AX

1 First consider if really sharp objects and drinking beer go together

2 Whack cap off with ax

3 Try not to break glass bottle

4 Drink

5 Do not go back to chopping wood

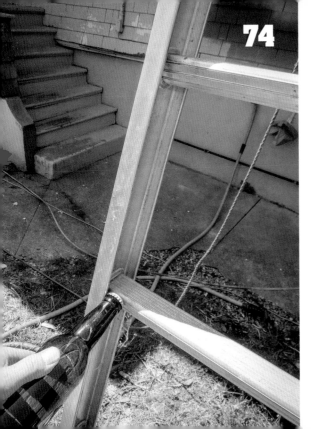

LADDER

1. Get off ladder
2. Place cap between step and rail
3. Press down
4. Drink
5. Don't get back on ladder

CROSSWALK BUTTON

1. Press button and wait for light to change
2. Place cap in between button and metal cover
3. Pry off cap
4. Wait for light to change for right to walk
5. Drink

STOP SIGN

1. Stop and find a stop sign
2. Place cap in between support pole and sign
3. Press down to remove cap
4. Drink
5. Go

NEWSPAPER VENDING MACHINE

1 Pretend to read the headlines

2 Place cap in coin return

3 Press down

4 Drink

PAY PHONE

1. Yes, they still do exist
2. Pick up phone and pretend to talk
3. Place cap in coin return
4. Pry off cap
5. Check coin return for loose change
6. Drink
7. Place receiver back on phone rest

PARKING METER VENDING MACHINE

1. Place cap in receipt opening
2. Press down
3. Don't forget to get parking ticket
4. Drink

AUTOMATIC TELLER MACHINE

1 Place cap in cash dispenser slot

2 Pull up

3 Drink

4 Take out cash to buy more beer

PARK BENCH

1. Take a walk in the park
2. Wedge cap between wood slats
3. Pry off cap
4. Sit back down on bench
5. Drink

BARRICADE

1. Place cap in between metal frame
2. Press forward to remove cap
3. Drink
4. Stay away from hole in the ground

BACKHOE

1. Find a large piece of construction equipment
2. Locate a metal edge
3. Pry off cap
4. Drink
5. Do not operate backhoe while drinking

BULLDOZER TREAD

1. Finish knocking down building
2. Stop bulldozer
3. Place cap in between track
4. Pry off cap
5. Drink
6. Do not operate bulldozer while drinking

DUMPSTER

1 Welcome to a giant bottle opener

2 On something this big it has to work anywhere

3 Pry off cap on a clean surface

4 Drink

PORT-O-POTTY

1. Your lucky day: start with a six-pack of beer
2. Place cap in door latch
3. Pry off cap
4. Drink
5. Go inside Port-O-Potty and pee
6. Repeat steps 2 to 5 five more times
7. Don't forget to wash your hands

URINAL

1. Which comes first: opening a beer or needing to pee?
2. Stand squarely in front of urinal
3. Wedge cap into plumbing fixture
4. Pry off cap
5. Drink

BATHROOM STALL HINGE

1 Find yourself in bathroom because you've already had a few

2 Place cap in door hinge

3 Press down

4 Don't forget to wash your hands

5 Go back to party

6 Drink

TRUCK LATCH

1. Wedge cap under lock latch
2. Press down
3. Drink

MOTORCYCLE

1. Place cap in cylinder block

2. Press down

3. Drink, but don't drive

LAUNDRY DRYER

1. Collect one month's worth of dirty laundry

2. Wash and dry clothing

3. While waiting, stick cap of beer in dryer door hinge

4. Drink

5. Now put on some clean underwear

ELEVATOR

1. Place cap in between door and cab frame
2. Pull back
3. Drink
4. Don't forget to push a floor button

TIKI HEAD

1. Find tiki head
2. Place cap in mouth
3. Press down
4. Offer your new friend a sip
5. Drink

SHOPPING CART

1. Go to supermarket and buy beer for party

2. Decide you need a beer right now

3. Place cap in metal frame

4. Pry off cap

5. Drink

6. Please return cart to store

DOG COLLAR

1. Take best friend out for walk
2. Grab beer from fridge
3. Tell dog* to stay
4. Place bottle cap in D-ring of collar
5. Pry off cap
6. Continue walk
7. Drink

* This will not work with a Chihuahua.

FIRE HYDRANT

1 Locate hydrant that's on virtually every block

2 Follow arrow to "OPEN"

3 Place cap between hydrant top and nut

4 Pull up

5 Drink

FIRE ALARM

1 Place cap behind metal frame

2 Gently pry off cap

3 Do not pull fire alarm

4 Drink

HANDCUFFS

1. Wake up and wonder how you got yourself handcuffed (drinking too much beer?)

2. Pick lock to uncuff one hand (try a paper clip)

3. Position single strand through double strand of cuff

4. Pry off cap between double strand

5. Drink

POLICE CAR

1. Make sure nobody is in the car
2. Make sure again that nobody is in the car
3. Place cap in trunk lid
4. Press down
5. Don't drink
6. RUN
7. Drink
8. Don't get caught

BOOK COVER

1. Buy a copy of this book

2. Grab bottle securely under cap with one hand

3. With other hand, rest spine of book on top of thumb and under cap

4. Pry off to pop cap off

5. Read book to learn the other ninety-nine ways

Index by Method

Acknowledgments

Thanks to: Patricia Anderson, anonymous hand model, Paul Bartnik, Justine Busby, Nicole Carr, Adam Clark, Joey Clark, Jim Crouch, Hal Drellich, Mark Einhaus, Fred Elliott Jr., Chris Gioarelli, Wayne Gsell, Desire Guensh, Sean Kalley, Paul Kassar, Dave Kolar, John Kolar, Joanna Lester, Victoria Lewis, Jim Lindsay, Frank Milan, Chris Nukauce, Lev Tsypin, Steve Wuestoff, Tracy Wymer, Brian Yoder, and Patrick Zahn.

A special thanks to Adrienne Rosado and Nancy Yost. They are my literary agents, if what I'm doing here is really literature.

Mom, thanks for paying for college.

About the Author

Brett Stern is an industrial designer who has several patents on surgical instruments, medical implants, and robotic manufacturing systems. He is also the inventor of Beer Chips® snack foods, wherein he figured out how to get beer into potato chips without making them soggy. He drinks beer and lives in Portland, Oregon.